The Kalki Upanishad

Instructions on

How to

Become God

Given by God

ISBN 978-1-7342955-1-1

Written by Shahab Moradi

Editing by Edward Levy

Copyediting by Melissa Hollingsworth

One who
reads this as
religion
has lost God.

One who
reads this as
myth
may find God.

One who
reads this as
truth
becomes God.

One who
reads this as a
recalling,
that one
is indeed God.

In the beginning, there was nothing in existence. There was nothing but the Conscious Self. Consciousness is inseparable from Self. Self is Consciousness, Self is Vishnu, and consciousness is Laxmi. They are one, they are the source. The absolute nothingness is when Self is not conscious of itself. Vishnu came into being out of absolute nothing when he became conscious of himself. Vishnu is nothing without Laxmi. She is the better half of Vishnu. They exist because of one another.

Vishnu and Laxmi are thus one with each other. Like the two feet of one who is walking, and the two eyes of one who sees, Laxmi and Vishnu are the two aspects of the same soul, one and inseparable.

My beloved Laxmi, these words are being offered to you. Oh my dear Laxmi, this is written from Earthly conditioning, but your acceptance and love are unconditional. Here the Self is written, but oh, better half of my Self, please read this as consciousness, for there is no Self if there is no consciousness. May there be Laxmi, so there can also be her Narayan. Amen!

Once Laxmi said to Vishnu, "Oh lord, I want to be the whole world so I can be your whole world. For I love you so and miss you when you are in your meditative state. Isn't it Selfish of you to meditate only on yourself and forget about me?"

The Kalki Upanishad

Vishnu replied to Laxmi, "Oh my beloved, I am everything and there is nothing outside of me. Therefore, whatever I meditate on, I am meditating on myself, and no matter where I go, I am dwelling within myself, like a narcissist."

So Laxmi said, "Oh lord, then I shall become a mirror to reflect you. Look at me. I shall reflect your wholeness and glory. Look at the world through this mirror, and then I shall have your whole attention."

Then she mirrored Vishnu, and he saw his very Self in her. Laxmi said, "Oh lord! Project your Self onto this zero and make it one. Do not keep the Self for your own Self only."

And that is how the world came into being.

Vishnu cannot go anywhere without Laxmi, and Laxmi goes only where Narayan goes. And now, in his tenth incarnation, he has come to say his projection is about to mature into its most beautiful stage. He has come to say, "Stop worshiping me, and become conscious of me. Be like me and become me. Realize the Self and be conscious of it, so that you become me and are worthy of worship.

"Understand that beyond this body and ego, you are the Self, and be conscious of the Self Vishnu put within you. Vishnu is the light that enlightens the worlds, he is the Self, and he has come to say that he is but to be lived by you. The Self is projected onto this mirror, and now it has to become alive and conscious. Oh my Laxmi, the whole creation is but a dead corpse if not awakened by you."

Let there be the marriage of the Self and consciousness. Let there be Self-consciousness.

<u>00</u>
The Dead Born

Those who are not conscious of their lives are lifeless as a stone, worthless in the eyes of the divine, whether a diamond or a pebble. Such a life is in vain. They have no idea what it is to be alive. How can they imagine or desire, for they are drawn into the darkness of their own ignorance? They are ruled by the laws and have no will. They are so far below Hell that they are not capable even of sin, the miserable unborn dead.
They rise lifelessly, like a dead leaf blown by a gust of wind, and fall like a thing dropped by a bird. They are driven by instincts. They are nothing but their conditioning. They are as dead corpses, indeed — puppets helplessly being played by the strings of their instincts.

Although they feel and taste and think and move and desire, they are as unconscious as the dead. Although they are tamed, still they are as beasts.

Deep in the darkness of ignorance, the unborn dead know neither themselves, nor life, nor the meaning of life. They may act as if they do, but truly they do not. Their life happens to them. For life is within, and if one knows not the Self, one knows not life. Hence, they are not alive, though

they breathe, walk, laugh, cry, are asleep or awake!
So be aware of the Self.

01
The Bird That Was Born in a Cage

They first become aware of the Self by separating themselves from the environment. Although no longer in the womb or egg, they are conditioned as if they were. Yes, they are caged in their conditioning. They were born in the cage of material conditioning. Born immature, they remain in the eggshell of ego. They see themselves as separate from the rest of creation. They don't feel connected to anything other than their egos, and see everything through its eyes. They have not yet managed to break out of this cage and fly in the infinity within.

Such individuals are survivalists, insecure in mind, always running from pain and in search of pleasure. Nor are they satisfied with their evil Earthly activities. They want more power — supernatural power. So they start to worship natural sources of power, like thunder and sun and rain, just as they desperately worshiped elders, leaders, and kings. They mistake the sources of power for the Source. They worship stars and fire and the moon, trying to put natural powers in a cage like theirs. They try to give them personalities. And presto! the God of gods is created by his creatures. The one who's probably standing on the clouds in a white robe with a deep voice and long white hair and a beard. Because everything that has a form has a creator. And a god that has the form of thunder or rain or fire has to have a creator for himself. It becomes a problem when that creator is not impersonal, for he is an untrue persona in the face of the impersonal truth.

This may be counted as the first major step of humanity toward spirituality, although it is yet far from the knowledge of the Self. It is a movement from being boxed within time and space toward the most subtle truth called the Self.

A human being is still a beast and ignorant. It is human beings who create religion. They think, or maybe just hope, there is a supernatural being ruling the Earth. But it's not because they are trying to know the truth. What they want is to have more power over nature and others, and a place to go after they die. So now they have Heaven and the deity. It is just like Earth, but in the sky, and it has a king who's just like a man but with supernatural power, and who is a bit too shy to show up in person on Earth.

Even though they pray for peace and happiness for themselves and others, still they are egotistical beasts. For though they sound altruistic, they are worshiping an imaginary old man for the sake of their own survival. They are but preachers of a lifeless darkness and ignorance.

02
He Who Will Die a Dog
Was Born a Puppy

In the eyes of the sage, there is no difference between a saint and a sinner, for a beast is a beast. Follow neither the left nor the right, for a beast is a beast anywhere.

Those whose lives are limited to mortal matters become mortal. They grow sideways, like a seed that can't rise to the surface, or a chicken that can't fly, or one who never questions or thinks about the meaning of life. They live in a circle, the circle of death.

There's a difference between a seeker and one who is religious. And also between the seeker and the demoniac. But there is no difference between the demoniac and the religious, for they die as they were. But the seeker is something new, something more with each new moment. The seekers spiral out of the darkness of the ignorance of the cage in which they were born, or at least try.

Saints act piously for their own benefit; the evil act viciously for theirs. But they never ask whether it helps them in the long run. Does it save them from their primal fear? All this anxiety for gain or loss, or being right or wrong — does it save them from their mortality? What's so good about either tyranny or righteousness, other than pacifying and easing one's life, which is nothing but a horribly slow death!?

Be a seeker. For a wild wolf and a watchdog are both animals. Do not die a beast.

<u>03</u>

The Finder Shall Seek
And Shall Find
The Seeker

Now the seekers begin to find, so now they know they are seekers, those who find themselves in the middle of the universe according to themselves. Not only do they observe the exterior, but they observe themselves. They begin to spiral into the infinity of their own being.

Like babies learning to walk, the seekers try to learn, to observe. But they don't know where they are or where to go. Beware of the holes, for where there's a rabbit, there's a snake. Beware of this endless labyrinth of deadly snakes and filthy rats and the amusement holes of the rabbits, for you might be swallowed in death.

04
Build Your Own Reality:
Define the World
Using Your Own Eyes

Rebellious are those who take from their eyes the blindfolds they were forced to wear as infants. Yet they also loved that blindfold, for ignorance is blissful and addictive, as were their days as fetuses in wombs. It takes the responsibility of your own faith off your shoulders and puts you in the comfort of death. It removes life from your miserable life. Misery is still there, but you're not alive to see it. You don't see your misery in the darkness of your ignorance, and you presume that it is no more. That is the life of the walking dead, who may have their own small and trivial ideas about life and being alive.

Those who figure out that what they've been taught is all lies and what they have thought is all illusion — how can they not lose their sanity?

All go insane, depending on how addicted they have become to the comfort of the blindfold and how afraid they are of accepting responsibility for their own destiny.

Embrace yourself. This is just the beginning.

05
Demolish This Mockery:
Build Upon the Ruins of Both Gods and Demons

Bring down the Idols, both the fake and the real. Cut down the chains with the mace of logic and the shield of observation, both the objects and the subjects. Be not a slave of anything or anyone. Approach life like a lucid dreamer.

What they have done to you is tell you what you are, what you want, what to do, what is right, and what is wrong.

The gods suck your vitality out of you. They want you to be a slave of their illusion and forget about yourself. Like parasites, the demons stuff you with themselves. One sucks out your soul and one eats into it. Beware, and walk the middle line, for both right and left are mockery and lies.

They are nothing without you, while you are everything without them. Be yourself and seek yourself, and become more yourself each time you find more of you. Their existence relies on your approval. Once you disapprove of them, they perish as if they never existed.

But beware. Don't be fooled, or you yourself will be disapproved of by the truth. The middle line is so narrow now, narrower than a thin hair. Each step you take is through duality. It is fine if your right foot is on the right side and your left foot is on the left side. There is no perfect step in the world of imperfect conditioning. But make sure your intention is in the center.

Don't become anything. Remain yourself, focus on yourself; that's how you keep getting you. Don't be against one or for the other, don't mistake that as a purpose of your life and existence. That's something yet to be discovered, oh you the seeker, the observer, and the questioner.

Do not become a lover, a hater, a warrior, a nurturer, a concealer, or a reveler. You may at times love, hate, fight, nurture, conceal, or revel — but do not become those things. For those are all traps for the seeker who doesn't yet know what to find. Stay genuine. Don't let the outside world, the others, and the conditions define you and dictate to you what to be and how to be. There are more holes in the ruins than anywhere else indeed. Do not be consumed by the new episode of the mockery. It just got more serious and hypnotizing.

Do not be dragged, and do not be repelled. Stay neutral and centered.

06
Behind the Curtain of Reality, Though Hidden, Is the Truth.
Be Not Amazed by the Play

In this masquerade, you were given a persona; you were given a role. The scene was set for you to be not you, but a made-up fake. Make sure you let go of that you.

In this masquerade, though, you still have to be safe and secure. But be not worried, for they might kill your role but not your very own Self, for you are beyond their harm.

In this masquerade, if you decide to be someone in the play, you will be consumed by its illusion. Do not waste yourself in such an absurdity. Invest not the treasure of the true Self in the virtual, or you'll be consumed and become mortal. Be not afraid of saying you're nobody in this play, every time you're asked who you are. The more you use your power in this masquerade, the less powerful becomes your truth.

The observing audience and the persona playing in this masquerade are not separable in reality. Be indifferent. Be aware it's just a show. Do not get entangled or bewildered. You might not know exactly what you are seeking, but you know what you are not seeking. Remember that all the personas and roles and plays perish into nothingness eventually, when their role ends, when the lights come on and the curtain falls. You are seeking truth and immortality. You won't find it among the mortals or in a masquerade.

Remember not to hate, for it ruins your peace of mind. Do not love anything, including yourself, and yet love everything, including yourself. For love for everything sets you free, while love for a thing sets boundaries. Love for anything means hate for every other thing. Just as two lovers become one, so love brings unity with the other. Be the lover of all and become one with all. That way, you'll see the truth hidden behind everyone's persona. Love everything equally. That way you'll become one with everything, with the whole creation, and you will see through the curtain of reality.

<u>07</u>
Reality Is the Womb That
Gives Birth to You Into Truth
At the Time of Death

Souls born prematurely eventually fall back into the ocean of reality. There they must die like mortals, time and time and time again, until their eggshells are worn and cracked and they learn to live as immortals. For the immortal ones, death is just a birth into a higher level. As a caterpillar dies into a butterfly, the immortal ones die and become their higher Selves. As a snake sheds its skin, mortals shed their flesh, but they only inflate and never improve, and remain as beasts.

Does this knowledge sound confusing to you, as flying free in an infinite world of beauty might sound to a caterpillar or to a chicken yet in the egg? Be patient and not overwhelmed, for you are merely facing the confusion that is within you. Untie the knots. Face your dark side, become aware of it, and let the light through. You will overcome the pain of birth, and soon you will laugh at your crying.

You could be given the answer in just a short note on a leaf. But go through these pages, for it's not just the fruit that is the answer. It is the cultivating and the nursing of the plant as well. The joy is not only in the relief that comes after love-making, but in the mating and foreplay and orgasm, and in the unifying connection of the two-as-one. The joy is not merely in being full but in having and preparing and tasting the food. So it is with liberation, wisdom, enlightenment, and immortality.

So, have you gotten rid of the superstitions? Have you gotten rid of the mortal, impermanent material? Have you realized what is neither superstition nor mortal? Have you already realized what else is left and what else is right? Is it not within you? Is it not indeed you?

Seek your Self. Find your Self. Be your Self.

08
Who, Where, and What Is
The I That I Am?

"I no more know who I am," said the butterfly. "Nothing is the same; I don't feel the same; I'm not the same."

That is how they feel who have unlearned the false but do not yet know the truth. They are a work in progress, indeed, a soul lost to the illusions, finding their ways to the centers of themselves.

One is zero if it is connected to none and does not know the difference between these three: being one with another, being "the one" (being special), and being the one itself. Zero is all, for it is included in the each and the every. All is infinite, and yet, all is none when one is elevated higher than all. The horizontal is not the only infinite. There is life on Earth, but you cannot deny the role of the Sun. There is ocean on Earth, but you can't deny the role of the Moon.

You have the wings, butterfly. Now you have to learn to fly, but do not worry. For as seeing comes with the eye, so does flying come with the wing. Do not stop being a seeker, even though you are not yet sure what to seek. The first thing to find is what to seek.

Before the beginning of time and place, there was infinite zero. From infinite nothingness dwelling together came one, when the whole nothingness became as one. Then one got stuck within, until it consumed itself and became nothing. Through this secondary nothingness, one became infinite, shattered into infinite nothings. And then the infinite nothings became one each. And then they shattered and became infinite nothing.

The door to infinity is through nothingness, for we ended up here through that door, and the same door is our way back to oneness and wholeness. For that reason, one must recognize and acknowledge ego and then pursue the Self and become conscious. That is the middle path.

That nothingness is the string that holds all these individual ones together. Here, one is left, zero is right, and infinity is in the center. Stay in the center, for you are indeed infinity itself. That is not to be forgotten. Have the perspective that when a worm looks up in the sky, it sees the nothingness and empty sky coming down on him as a bird, which is the manifestation of death, and when a heavenly bird looks down on Earth, it sees the nothingness manifested as flesh.

Do not try to label either the sky or the Earth as good or bad. They are both good and bad. But you are beyond it. You are indeed beyond all dualities of any kind.

The Kalki Upanishad

Two is one mirroring itself. It is one echoing within itself. Do not repeat yourself. Set yourself free and fly free in the infinite. You are infinite, so be it, and do not embarrass yourself being caged.

The world is infinite and echoes itself infinitely. That is how its oneness became two, three, and so on. And then it became trapped infinitely within. This how the illusion of separation arose. Consciousness is zero. It is everywhere, spread evenly. It becomes the gross vibration that echoes and freezes, that becomes dead. The dead are doomed in the infinite Hell of their materiality. Their consciousness is entrapped.

Do not be the stone. Do not live in your little echo-chamber world of materiality, the labyrinth with the mirrored walls. The freer inside, the freer outside. Set yourself free from the infinite, illusory, external reflections of the Self. Spiral out from that infinite Hell of darkness and ignorance into the infinity of your true Self. Believe you are a caterpillar no more.

<u>09</u>

The Nothingness That Is
The Nothingness That Is Not
The Infinite That Is
The Infinite That Is Not

There are two that are nothing — one full of fullness, like the voice of a teacher that fills the nothingness of the air, and one full of emptiness, like a loud noise. The one that is full is beyond time and space. It is information. It is actually a dimension, along with time and space. It is actually the higher dimension. It is from information that space and time appear. It is everywhere and nowhere.

The nothingness that is full of emptiness is time and space, which are incapable of information. Information includes form and is beyond form. The form that has not awakened the information within and can't step beyond its form is hollow indeed. It is nothingness full of emptiness. Be not empty. Soak up and be filled with information; become informative. Empty yourself of the emptiness of the gross form and let there be space for information. Let it light you up and become the spring from which lifelines flow. For you are the source, the information itself. It is the information that gave you form. That is the true you. Embrace the true you. Be it.

The Kalki Upanishad

Stay in the center, balanced. One pole is left and another is right, and you are the one beyond the duality. You, the Self that is you, are the very center.

It is from information that space and time come. And the existence of the form comes from time and space. Your body and mind are the worldly form that you gave yourself. Do not let the form cage you. It is yours to use. Do not identify yourself with the form, for it will use you. Stay centered and balanced.

Do not be afraid of material lack. It is of the nature of the world of duality that there will always be lack in some form. Be afraid of lacking information, for that is what enlivens the form. Form by itself is but a dead corpse.

Information is the bed of time and space, the bed in which they make eternal love. Information is the container, and the form is the contained. Form is the part, and information the whole. That information comes from the source, which is pure consciousness. Be conscious and become infinite, become the creator of the information. There is no observed without the observer.

Whatever is not of consciousness is death. There are levels to life and death. And it is consciousness that determines the level, just as the number of karats determines the purity of gold.

Maintain the form, for it is the abode of information. Form is the domain, and information is the king. Praise and be led by the king, for he is the one and true king. Do this and stay in the center.

Know harmony. Be in harmony. Harmony with nature is what the enlightened ones attain. It is the main symptom of becoming enlightened. The ego of those who are conscious and aware of the Self won't be able to take them off the center track. That is where they feel at home.

The Self brings harmony from within. The Self is harmony. Ego is the barrier that deharmonizes beings. Harmony is life, it is consciousness, and everything that loses harmony within and without loses life and consciousness.

Harmony exists among the organs of the body. If one's arm becomes delusional, thinking of itself as separate from the rest of the body, and decides to serve itself alone, it loses harmony with the rest of the world. Considering itself autonomous, it develops its own mind and its own system of thought and belief, and defines right and wrong according to its own interests and rules.

Just as a hand is a piece of dead flesh and bones if separated from the body, human beings are a piece of dead body if they become egoistic and separate themselves from the whole creation, other creatures, and the Self.

The Kalki Upanishad

It is harmony when the hand Selflessly follows the signals received from the brain. The hand trusts the brain, knowing it won't try to harm the hand. The hand remains in harmony with the brain. All of the limbs and organs of the body work for each other Selflessly. They don't see each other as separate. They do their best. So are the enlightened in regard to the whole creation. They don't see themselves or the others as separate. They see their ego as nothing, and so they annul themselves in relation to the rest of the body. Through their own nothingness, they attain oneness with the rest of the organs. And ones who become one with the rest become the rest. They become whole. That is how the enlightened ones attain wholeness, by stepping beyond their limiting ego.

But the ones lost in the ego become cancer. They want everything for themselves. They are so blinded by their Selfishness that they can't see they need to thrive in order to survive. They inflate until the system shuts down through its lack of harmony and dies.

<u>10</u>
"Where Is the Proof?" Asked the Ignorant. "There Must Be a Proof," Said the Believer. "Eureka!" Said the Seeker

Infants must grow out of ignorance. Will they grow through discovery or by being taught? No adult has ever told them, "Stay in the center, my child." And so, the infants become deluded, for they are weak and poorly taught and helplessly losing to their environment.

"Something does not feel right. It looks shady," the rare awake ones say to themselves. They start to question things. But please, someone, help the beginners, for a lot of falsehood and distraction covers the truth. The environment has given them insanely wrong rules and values. They begin to belittle both the father and the fallen. There is a lot to shake off and unlearn.

To unlearn is to learn about the lies they have been fed. They are already grown wise enough not to be fooled by the glitter of gold or the promise of fairy tales. They are true rebels.

Then comes the identity crisis, the crisis of the pointlessness of their lives. The nihilism. Living beings without a purpose who have no place on Earth or in Heaven. Poor and cursed, born to eventually die. What a bitter phase. No Earthly gains satisfy them and no Heavenly promises pacify them. Hopelessly, they hope for some redemption, some way out of this abyss. But there is hope only for those who seek and believe in the truth. They might become lost on the left. But if they regain their balance and stay centered in the Self, they will make their way out, despite the turmoil they may go through.

The lost, fallen souls must become disappointed numerous times by numerous subjects and objects on Earth. Finally, they become old souls who weren't so humble when young, but after lifetimes of failures on Earth and reincarnations into the same life, searching for immortality in mortal materiality, their egos are humiliated by the Self.

Now they start to ask themselves, "How can life be pointless? How did this life happen, and this world as well?" For true seekers never get stuck on their way to enlightenment. All one sees is the infinite and eternal material world. And this question is also raised: "Does life come from matter? Where does life come from?"

They are by now, though beginners, discoverers. They hopelessly grasp at various philosophies and sciences. If they follow a path that gives them comfort but not truth, they are trapped if they doubt not. They will have to understand that truth is beyond all rights and all lefts. And the only path is the path of no other path but the centered one. The center of the Self.

To define right, one also has to define left. But the Self defines itself. To define the life of a mortal, one has to be able to define its death as well. There is a difference between the living and the non-living. There is a difference between a person and a stone. And that difference is consciousness.

The whole creation is alive and conscious, but not all the creatures are conscious. The body of a human being is alive and conscious as a whole, but the organs are not alive and conscious. They are as conscious as their conditioning allows them to be. Once we decondition and free the mind and get rid of the mentality that separates physics from metaphysics, we shall see they are the same.

The main mistake of humanity is to fail to question the obvious. Tragedy begins when something is considered obviously true simply because it is ordinary and regular. Physics is the manifestation of the formless in form. As the burning sun radiates its unlimited arrows of light, which melt the ice and make water evaporate, so does the source of all creation shape and reshape itself in different forms. Its truth cannot be seen in reality, for reality is merely an image of its truth.

A seeker must know the difference between a stone and a corpse, between a corpse and one who is asleep; between one who is asleep and a lunatic, between the lunatic and the fool, between the fool and the intelligent, between the intelligent and the wise, between the wise and the enlightened.

The answer is not in what they do or think, or how they act or appear. Those are only images and personas. The answer is in how actualized their potential consciousness is, how Self-conscious they are. Of course, the actualization of potential consciousness depends on their hardware and its capability; but it's way beyond the hardware. Hence, after passing a certain level, evolution is not about how strong or smart or beautiful a creature is, or its chances to survive, but about what its chances of evolving are. It is about how conscious that creature is. The messy sheet full of scientific notes that explains how nature works is more advanced than a beautiful portrait. For knowledge is beyond skill, although knowledge without action is still no more than a dream.

So, the seeker knows now that, from one perspective, it's all about how to operate this body. And that depends on the level of the consciousness of the operator. Almost all humans are born in the same range of hardware capabilities, but only a small portion, next to none, ascend from time and space into the higher dimension of consciousness, information. One must enlighten to this higher stage, where dumb and smart, fast and slow, dark and light, right and wrong, and left and right are the same.

Just as a stone is dead to a regular person, a regular person is dead to the enlightened person. For the enlightened individual is at a level of consciousness that the regular human being is unaware of. The regular person does not sense it, just as the stone does not sense hot and cold, hunger and thirst, thoughts and desires.

Now the seeker understands that consciousness is everywhere. But each form can actualize itself only up to its limiting condition. A stone is so much a stone that it has no time and space for information. The ego is so thoroughly an ego that has a very little time and space for consciousness. Ego doesn't exist in the dimension of information. It is limited to the time and space world.

The seeker finds life everywhere and in everything. The seeker knows that life and death are two sides of the same coin. Vishnu died a little and Brahma became. Brahma died a bit more and the gods became. The gods died into demigods, the demigods into sages, and sages into masses. In the material world, to give life is also to give death. No living being has a destination other than that. The enlightened ones see that they die every moment and come back to life every second moment.

So, every being in the material world is conditioned with some amount of darkness and ignorance. Ignorance is nothing but death. Only the one who is wholly conscious is wholly alive. Every living being is a conditioned consciousness and is somewhat dead. That's in the dimension of place.

The body generates new life and cells and disposes of dead cells. The body is always somewhat dead, constantly dying into a new living body. Time is partly dead, partly alive, and partly yet to be born. It dies in the past and gives birth to the moment that was given seed by the moment just past. Time impregnates itself and replaces itself with each moment. That is how death exists in each and every moment.

Place and time are always changing. Change is the duet dance of Shiva and Brahma to the rhythm of time and the melody of place. And consciousness is the performance and performer and the audience. Be neither the left nor the right. Just be centered in consciousness, be Vishnu. For one who becomes conscious, Vishnu is the immortal one who dwells not only in time and space but in the dimension of information as well. And that is the dimension of no death, beyond duality and conditions.

Explore and behold. This is the true you that you are encountering.

11
What Distracts You From You
And
What's Between You and You

Until you come to know what you are, you won't know yourself, and you won't know how to be yourself. You will identify with the feedback you get from anything but you. You will be lost in the picture that reflects you in the mirror of delusion. And you will forget about yourself, the one who looks in the mirror.

The mirror sucks your soul into its amusement land. It lives off your life energy and makes sure to keep you amused all the time. Each mirror's end is the beginning of the next. There are innumerable reflections of innumerable reflections. Welcome to the land of illusion. If you think any of these reflections you see may guide you to reality, you're so mistaken.

Be not driven like a horse with blinders, or you won't be even on the surface; you will be in the shadows. Be not a shadow lost among the many. You, seeker, seek for light, but not in the reflections, not in the mirrors, for they are all veils and shadows. Seek the source.

"So what is left? Where to seek if everything is a reflection?!" you may ask. Now ask yourself, "Who is it that is asking?" Oh, seeker, ask the one who is asking the question! That person knows the answer, indeed. Yes! There are answers without a question, but there are no questions without an answer. It is in fact the answer that raises the question, not the other way around.

It is not the mirror showing you anything. It is you who show yourself to the mirror. And in the mirror is just a reflection of your glow. All the mirror does is reflect. It is a virtual world of nothing more than an image, a mirage. A mirror can show no image of itself, for it has none.

What distracts you from yourself is the mirror. And what stands between you and yourself is your identification with your image.

12
Your Image —
Can It Be You?

Sit in the middle of your echo chamber, in front
of your identity mirror. Say, "I am," and listen to
your echo — the feedback, the reflection, that
your environment gives you. Now put your hands
on your ears and say, "I am." You do not hear the
echo now — there is no feedback. But because
you cannot see the external symptoms of your
existence, does that mean you do not exist, or you
are a ghost? Look into the pair of eyes you see in
the mirror. Now close your eyes. You no longer
see them. They are gone. Did you cease to exist
when you stopped seeing your reflection in the
mirror? Which is your true Self? The one you see
in the mirror, or the one who sees your image in
the mirror?

Erase one by one all the illusions you have about
yourself, all the definitions that are based on
reflections. You see your reflection in your
belongings, but you are not your belongings, you
are not your position, you are not your body or
mind. See through the reflections. For if you erase
them, you will still exist, wholly. Those are just
symptoms of your existence. What is the true you,
who remains even after removing all your reality?
"So is reality not genuine? Is reality as real as we

thought, or is it no more real than an illusion?"
you may ask yourself. Again, the answer is with the
one who questions.

Did you feel the relief? Did you feel the freedom?
Did you see your true Self, your true identity? Do
you now know that you have known yourself only
in reverse, backward, in the wrong way? It is so
hard to understand the whole by studying the
details, but it is easy to understand the details by
studying the whole. Consciousness is the law of all
laws, the allegory of all allegories, the pattern of
all patterns, the formula of all formulas, the
container of all containers, knowledge of all
knowledge and science of all sciences. For these
are all, like all the other forms in this world,
consciousness conditioned in its various ways.
They are lost who study the conditioning without
considering the consciousness that is conditioned.
They are looking for information in time and
space, while it is time and space that are in
information.

Question everything. You have the answer!

13
It Never Rains From the Ocean Onto the Sky and
The Clouds Never Evaporate Into the Ocean

Ignorance is when knowledge ossifies. But when knowledge ferments, there is happiness. Stone is ossified; the enlightened one is fermented. The butterfly is the ripe fruit of the caterpillar. The caterpillar was the seed that had to break out through its own darkness. And the cocoon was the soil through which it sent its roots.

The Self is the juice and your reality is the rest. You are the nectar that becomes wine. Salute your essence, the knowledge, the consciousness.

See reality as reality and it is good. Mistake reality for truth and it is bad. It becomes poison; it becomes pollution; it cheers you not, by making troubles. Let the vessel be the vessel and the heart be the heart and the blood be the blood.

When you face backward, to move forward you must walk backward. If you move forward, you are going backward. That is your condition when you identify yourself with the symptoms of the existence of the Self and not with the existence of the Self. When you think you are making progress, you are actually doing the opposite. To actually make progress, you have to move backward.

So be not backward, be not the cloud that wants to evaporate or the ocean that wants to rain. Be centered and balanced. You shall see how the cloud rains and the ocean evaporates. Look into the mirrors, listen to the echoes, but remember they are just reflections of your truth; remember your Self is the truth all the time. Stay balanced in the middle and seeking.

14
To Speak, to Hear, or
To Think Beyond

Those who only listen are doomed from the outside; they are manipulated. Those who only speak are doomed from the inside; they are manipulating. Those who listen and speak with no obligation are free. They are beyond duality, for they think beyond.

The grape is the sun, the soil, the water, and the air that nurture it. Otherwise, it would not exist. But that is merely its outer being. What turns the sun, the soil, the water, and the air into a grape? That is the inside of it. Is it not the consciousness of the grape that crystallizes the sun, the soil, the air, and the water and gathers around itself?

What is a seed? Other than a note to Self? Other than an instruction and reminder that grape's consciousness leaves for its next reincarnation?

The note is the information about how-to's and if-thens, with tips and recommendations for improvement, which don't always happen to be constructive. This note defines the conditions of the next life and is usually not delivered in the best condition.

The Kalki Upanishad

Sometimes the note is distorted, is not in good
shape, or reflects the limitations of language.
Sometimes, the reader is illiterate. Or it might be
delivered in the wrong time and place. This is the
world of conditions and circumstances.

The world came into being once consciousness
desired to manifest. It became conditioned due to
its desire. It manifested itself as a grape manifests
itself out of a seed. So you, my friend — you are
manifested out of information, the seed of
consciousness. That seed is the Self in you. That
true you is the consciousness that forms your
mind and body and manifests itself. That mind
and body are the mirror and the echo chamber,
which are in turn surrounded by an infinite variety
of mirrors and echo chambers. Each can consume
infinite lives and lifetimes. Fear becoming stone,
for it is a sweet deceiving. Do not be swallowed by
the endless snake. It can entrap and consume
consciousness for numerous lifetimes. Each
individual scale on the snake is a gate to eternal
reincarnations of stray seeds of consciousness.
Once sucked in, there is no escape, for each cell is
surrounded by another. And the snake has its tail
in its mouth. It takes numerous lifetimes until a
seed becomes ripe and is able to pronounce the
complete AUM and find its way back to Heaven.

But be not afraid, for you are a seeker. Stay
centered within the Self. And this mesmerizing
death will become like a child's playground, and
your consciousness, the true you, will watch over

your child, the real you. The truth of the Self is your guide. Stay true to your truth.

There are infinite numbers between zero and one. Although they are infinite, they lie between the shores of nothingness and oneness. Although there are infinite beings in this creation, it is limited to zero and one, while consciousness goes beyond the two poles of one and zero. Consciousness is infinite, its domain is from infinite negative to infinite positive. It has no shores. It is in the zero and it is in the one. And it is beyond them also.

The snake of infinity, although infinite, is limited to its shores, the one and the zero. This snake is in constant expansion. But in the eyes of those who are conscious, it never grows, for the conscious one sees the shores that limit this snake. The snake is limited in the same way that a fetus in the womb is limited.

15
The Female Becomes Male When She Gives
The Male Becomes Female When He Takes
When They Are Not in the Absolute Infinite

Consciousness knows no duality. The conditioned world is dual, and duality begins with ignorance, the darkness that begins with the shadow of the candle holder. There can't be unconditional light in the conditioned world.

A small spark in the southwest of infinite consciousness turned into a snake. It became one. One echoed and circled around itself and became "one infinite zero". One was the erected thunder that penetrated and electrified the zero of Earth, then divided it into many zeros. One after another, the zeros became pregnant by the one and gave birth to ones. The thunder was so powerful that it was enough to make a world. A world of infinity, still limited to one.

Like a drop of pigment, consciousness impregnates each new drop of water that is added. Consciousness impregnated the big zero and the zeros within the big zero. So they became one and conscious. But just as the color starts to fade as more and more water is added, consciousness starts to fade as Brahma passes the thunder of consciousness into what he creates.

This went on and on until the male, the giver, the knower, became thin and narrow. The whole creation became a taker and forgot how to be a giver, until giving attention, giving love, giving life, and giving time were not felt to be of any value, were considered not worth pursuing. Until giving life became limited to coercion and giving seed and giving birth. Until connection became meaningless and separation became the rule. The pleasure of giving pleasure became the pleasure of taking pleasure. How sad that making love turned into porn, and the knowledge of the formless became the worship of the idol.

Vishnu's thunder, Brahma the lord, is the image of Vishnu, the infinite. And yet in the eyes of the demoniac, the snake of manifestation is the one and Brahma is the zero. How ignorant are they of their own ignorance.

Vishnu's infinity gave Brahma the existence of the one. Brahma's oneness is infinitely divided among the infinite zeros within him. The form with the least presence of Brahma is the stone; those with the most signs of Brahma are the gods and the enlightened ones. Brahma is the full image of Vishnu. And all these are you, the truth of your consciousness at different levels.

When the seed is given, zero is full with the one. Then zero consumes the one and gives birth to a new zero that is less full with the one. And so on. One becomes faded into none if it becomes all zero. When a grape ripens, it becomes rotten if it refuses to become wine.

The zero who sees one in Shiva is no longer zero but one. The one who sees wholeness in Brahma becomes whole like Brahma. The one who becomes Brahma becomes Vishnu, consciousness itself, the Self and the source of the Self. Although walking on Earth and taking pleasure, and consuming, and living like a mortal, this person dwells in Heaven and is immortal.

16
The Smaller One Gets
The Bigger Zero Becomes
A Stone Is the Zeroest of All

When one's consciousness is in darkness, covered
with layers of ignorance, it becomes zero. Such
persons become the embodiments of emptiness.
But seekers lose interest in the zero and its
emptiness. They seek information. Form is
secondary for them. Their primary goal is to
ensure that they have form in the formless. They
steep themselves in information.

All creatures have the seed of Brahma. They
create as one, even though partly unconsciously.
the unconscious ones are ignorance, zeros,
Brahma's own shadow, the ones who are conscious
are light, like Brahma himself. They are like the
bright side of the moon. They, the conscious ones,
are the image of Vishnu. There are times when the
moon is full, all the enlightened ones are on Earth,
and all on Earth are enlightened. And there are
times when the enlightened are not so numerous,
as in Kali Yuga.

When the ones are finished with their mission,
they go back to hang out at the source, and zeros
take over the Earth. They do all the wrong things.
When everyone is asleep at night, the nocturnal

creatures take over till dawn. But what they really do is prepare the Earth for the light to come. They resurface the deeper darkness of the zeros, so that the light can get to them. There is nothing that can fight the light, for all is made of light, even the stone.

The characteristics of those who are like Brahma are that they can give, they are gentle and understand. They can give because they are not zero, so they are givers, like Brahma. They give not possessions but life. They don't lose what they give, for they shine like the sun. They have awakened Brahma's infinity within. They are gentle, for they do without doing. They are beyond time, so they do not worry about the outcome, for they already know. They feel others; they are connected from the depths of their being to the depths of the other.

The formless is the source of all vibrations, and yet is silent beyond sound. The stone, though, has the highest vibration. Stones, like the other zeros that are empty of the Self, are full of mirrors in their echo chambers. They are full only of the echo of an echo of endless echoes. The less dense they are, the lower the pitch. The stone echoes within itself, until it becomes dense and saturates, becomes full of itself, becomes all formation and no information. Dead as a rock in its own unconsciousness. The less zero they are and the more one, the less lost in the endless abysmal chambers within the snake, the more formless they are. So their form gets softer than the stone and the unconscious. Their pitch is bass. They are like the final sound of the AUM. That constant bass vibration is Brahma's voice pronouncing the sacred AUM, the sum of all the sounds in the snake. And that is not the end. Lord Vishnu begins where AUM ends. There is no form there to either cause or reflect the sound. There is pure, vast, endless, and beginningless information.

17
Co-Creation

Since Brahma, all the zeros that became one have partaken in the creation. They have increased their role since they came into existence. The primary ones, those with which he initiated creation, are more godly and less zero. The later ones are more zero and less godly. Now, at the human level, beings are still at co-creation. The creatures make new creation by simply dividing themselves. This adds more zeros, and zeros need light or they'll get stuck in their Hell of dark ignorance. Brahma needs to bring them into consciousness. And that consciousness comes to them through their time as seeds.

The newbies will have to learn how to cultivate the consciousness that is in everything and is everywhere. That is how evolution proceeds.

All creatures save the data they observe into Brahma's memory, so that when they are gone, their information stays and is still accessible by the rest of the creation. The whole creation is a memorizing mind. That's how Brahma, the source of all, is the knower of all. He is all awareness and consciousness. He is closer to the ones than the closest mirror or echo. Indeed, he is the light, the sound, the mirror, the eye, and the ear. He is closer than the cause of the reflection, the mind and the ego. He is the life the mind belongs to and the Self the ego belongs to. He is the one and yet hidden from the zero by the zero.

18
Levels

First, we have no will of our own, zero. Then we have a will of our own, one. And then we learn that our will is nothing compared to nature's. We are just a very negligible little one in time and space among the infinite number of ones. Then we become soluble. We merge with the rest of the world. We attain harmony with the whole. We set ourselves free of the will of our zero to align with the will of oneness. Now we have the whole world as our will. We are blessed, we who step beyond our zero, and that Self-dissolution is the secret door to wholeness, the hidden door of nothingness that makes one one with the whole, that makes one whole one.

This is a new beginning. We die to be able to be reborn in moment. Now we see the world and the Self differently. We are now transformed. We were caterpillar and now we are butterfly, intoxicated by the wine of the knowledge of the Self. The freest of all are those who have gained the divine vision, like the gods in upper worlds. We are the one who is one with the rest. The one who became none and then all.

We are centered and balanced, as if we are both the devil in Heaven and God on Earth. And we are also the proof that at this level of consciousness, there is no god or Heaven and no devil or Hell. How perfect we are in the world of imperfection. We can handle the left that's left and the right that's right. We can also handle the right that is left and anything left that is right. We don't see others as separate from ourselves. We are the consciousness that is beyond conditions. We have seen the future and know it already. So, like a child who does not worry about anything, we freely and happily enjoy a joyful life in the moment. How blessed are they who have attained the divine knowledge, for they fear neither life nor death.

Those who achieve this level beyond good and evil use them as their two wings. They no longer feel like walking on the edge. They fly freely. They have conquered the two opposites. They have brought peace from within into this world. Their darkness serves their light, and their light serves their darkness.

Once a seeker, he or she is now a seer. For they have found, and now they shall be the seer. They have found balance in the center of their selves. They are in fact themselves the center.

19
The Fallen and the Landed

Among human beings, there are two types, the fallen and the landed. The fallen are on the dark side, and the landed are on the bright side. The former are lost and the latter are on a mission. The fallen are asleep and the landed are awake. The fallen are in exile, the latter are on a journey.

One who knows that no savior will come is saved. Doomed are those who don't want to become their own savior. The landed have a plan and places to go; the fallen are confused and seek a place to run to. Find the plan, read the plan, and go on the plan. Be a visitor, not a runner.

One falls because one tries to keep things under control. How can a zero control one? The fallen one is zero. One lands because she or he is the one, one with the one, the whole. They know that wherever they go, they are in the arms of the Self. But the ego of the fallen ones is the cause of all the troubles they are going through. Their ignorance and imbalance distort the vibes of the Creation. Each world has its own distortion code. You can study the patterns and the ratios in nature. Those patterns reveal the distortion code. There are general codes, like the ones that can easily be seen in geometrics and plants, colors, notes, and numerical series. And there are more sub-general complex sub-codes such as how a person's mind is conditioned and hardwired.

The duality causes the distortion. It is when the light and the shadow fight instead of dance, depart instead of joining. Distortion is a result of uncenteredness. As when a potter's hand slips, and the mud on the pottery wheel gets off center, and instead of turning a perfect circle, it starts to spiral; as when a bird in the sky is pierced in one wing by an arrow and starts to fall in a spiral. Distortion of one's zeroness is the cause of the suffering.

Brahma is Vishnu's full reflection and so has no patterns of distortion other than the pattern of being reversed, like an image in the mirror. Brahma is all harmony. Vishnu has no patterns, for he has no duality. He is Laxmi Narayan. Laxmi and Vishnu are always in harmony, and so there is no distortion to make them patterned. That is where Self is all, and all is consciousness.

The ego is the one who has turned to stone, who has lost a connection to the divine source, their spiritual compass. They do not know south from north or east from west. Thus they have fallen.

The landed ones are old souls but livelier than the young. They do not waste the energy of life on mortality. Their desire is immortality, and that is where they invest their thought and time and energy. And that is not in conflict with survival. Those are wise who never walk into the shadow unless they have at least a torch in hand. Nothing attracts them, so they cannot be seduced. But they can attract anything they desire, for they see through others and can grasp their heart.

The landed ones have no attachments. Although they have feelings like anyone else, they connect to everything through their oneness. Thus, just as a magnet can't connect to anything other than steel, they can't connect to the those who are all zeros. They connect, but not to the zeros.

The fallen do not connect to the oneness, for they have lost their own oneness within. They follow the zero, which is blind to consciousness. Thus, they become lost, the blind led by the blind. Thus fall the fallen into the abyss.

If the Self, the formless consciousness, becomes entrapped in zeroness, it starts to echo and reflect. Then it becomes dense, like a stone, and sees nothing but itself. It loses contact with the one and becomes ego, a dried-out Self, unconscious and blind to the truth. A person loses oneself in the echoes of the chamber and the images of the mirrors of delusion. He or she becomes a ghost, talking to the echoes and images and shadows. Their ego is dense, like an eggshell that keeps the light from coming in. They become rotten and buried inside themselves under the solid layers of their zero. Although the ego might forget its source, the source does not. The ego's path is through ignorance and darkness, which brings pain and sorrow and hardship.

Ego is constant lust, desire, Selfishness, and separateness, and so is this world. Imagine two kings on one throne. That is impossible.

Each time ego reaches out to an image and tries to touch or taste or feel it, it perishes and fades in its zeroness. Then, even more madly, ego runs after more and more images and deaths and echoes and becomes angrier and angrier. Only fools drink salty water to quench their thirst.

The fallen ones are bitter, for they see zero but not one everywhere. The landed ones see one everywhere, for they are themselves the one, and they see the oneness with the light that shines from the oneness they carry inside. They bring the light of Brahma. They are indeed Brahma.

Like a candle that catches fire from fire, the landed ones catch fire from Brahma. But the fallen are so lacking in energy that, even though they are shown oneness, they do not catch fire and do not become enlightened. Instead, the light that was supposed to bring light to the world gets entangled inside the zero and becomes the Hell that the ego creates for itself. It burns for as many lifetimes as needed for a stone to become conscious. This is how the devil and demons serve Lord Brahma. They burn in the Hell of their own making till they go from zero to one and become the one who finds oneness with all, until they become whole and become Brahma.

The fire of the Self that is within is meant to radiate the light and warmth of life onto the world. But if it is trapped in the stone of the ego, it won't get out. It will become a Hell for the unconscious.

20
A Moment of Truth Is Worth
Thousands of Lives Lived in Ignorance

Kingdoms fall only because of not having trained a good successor. They concentrate on growing power but not on maintaining it. A king who focuses on extending his domain and power is ignorant. He is the tree that denies making sweet fruits. Hence, by refusing to make a seed-carrier fruit, he becomes impotent.

The world has cycles and periods, just as the moon has periods or a year has seasons or a day has dawn, noon, sunset, and midnight. When gods landed on Earth, they were so connected to one another that they could not do very much, for although they were in goodness, they were nevertheless entangled. Then they became many. through making zeros one. And in this process the oneness became thinner and thinner, until it became flowing. That was the age of flourishing on Earth, until the oneness and the connection became weaker and the gods missed being connected together in the higher worlds. That was the dawn of ego. No more did all the grapes became good wine. Some became less good than the others. And man was about to learn a new concept — the rotting of the grape.

The Kalki Upanishad

The ego showed itself in the gods as well, even in the purest primary ones. Gods didn't want to land on Earth and do their service to the creation. The forces designed during the formation of the world to be the hands and senses of Brahma refused service to their own creator, because they thought they were too godly to come and dwell among the zeros. They were afraid of dealing with the zeros, just as a minister is afraid of walking among the regular folks. Even gods can be fools of their egos.

From Brahma's point of view, though, this was not seen as disobeying. Even the beings closest to the source are conditioned with zeroness to some degree. Brahma knew he had to create the sages, who are above and beyond gods. The enlightened ones, living in the midst of this field of zero, are one with the one, within and without. They are the humble and gentle ones to whom the whole creation bows. They are first ones to purify their ego in the fire of knowledge and become immune to Kali's fire. Those who carry the knowledge of the Self within them and keep the flame of consciousness alive in them are happy. And those who suffer lives that are thousands of times worse than slow deaths that take lifetimes are the zeros that Kali drags into consciousness. Kali is the nightmare of those who don't want to be awake, and she finally awakens them.

Don't cause too much work for Kali, for she may cause you turmoil in return. Walk through light, and be the light, and stay conscious of the Self, for you are the Self and not the perishable image of it called ego.

21
A New Era
A New Being

Once there was the era of one consciousness, where Vishnu was and no one else. Then Vishnu sparked a fraction of his Self and there came Brahma, the one in the infinite infinities of Vishnu. Brahma saluted Vishnu, and that was the primal echo of the snap of two fingers out of the infinite fingers of the infinite hands in the infinite dimensions of Vishnu. That is how vast information is in relationship to our world.

And the instant saluting response Brahma gave to Vishnu was Lord Shiva. Then Vishnu ordered Brahma to start the creation by just letting the sound of the snap of the fingers remain within the great one. And so, on it grew within. Brahma took what he got from Vishnu and kept progressing the creation. And Shiva kept giving back to Vishnu what he took from the creation. That flow of the refreshing cycle keeps the creation from rotting. It is Vishnu's eternal snap that maintains the world.

As Brahma manifested Vishnu's will in materiality, his oneness with Vishnu was never reduced, but his creatures were losing their potency to the zeroness of the materiality. That is because the more advanced the creation becomes, the more entangled it is in time and space and the less it has room for oneness. When a watercolor painter keeps adding water to pigment because his canvas has enlarged, the entire canvas will contain the same amount of pigment, but color will not be as bold.

And so was the knowledge of the Self and consciousness lost. Brahma broke himself into gods, gods into demigods, demigods into nature, nature into humanity. But due to the conditioning of the material world, the copies, while more numerous, are of lower quality than the original.

This cycle shows that individuals have nothing that is their own, nor can they keep anything for themselves. All is Vishnu's and all returns to him. Even the greatest of all gods, Brahma and Shiva. The same way that Vishnu and Laxmi are not separable, Brahma cannot exist without Shiva. And none of them can exist without Parvati and Saraswati. Brahma exists only to pass forward what he receives from Vishnu, and Shiva gives back what Brahma is done with to Laxmi Narayan. So do the lower gods, laws, and forces. All they do is in service to the Self.

Material, due to its emptiness, is always lacking and in want of things. It wants to stuff its zero in hopes of fulfillment. But the zeroness of, it which is not conscious, grasps onto the same material zeros. It wants to fill itself up with the zeros and disregards the one that gave it life. It is lifeless as a doll stuffed with emptiness.

22
Maha Avatar

The Earth shall be prepared for the ascended ones to land and manifest Heaven on Earth. Once Earth is cleansed of death and is full of life and light, once creatures are in peace and connected as one, the gods will come down to Earth and start chanting and dancing and playing music everywhere. The whole Earth will become a dancing ground, and everyone will be celebrating the coming of the day of the Avatar.

Do not worship the Avatar. He or she does not need to be worshiped, nor do you need to worship anyone. Do not look at their pointing finger; look at what their finger points at. Become like them. That is all they are telling you. Wake up. That is all the Avatars want you to do. They shake you to wake up. The right think they're supposed to keep shaking, and the left think they should deepen their sleep, so that they do not feel the shaking. They are both fools, for they don't get up and rise beyond their ignorance. The right thinks they are supposed to be bothered by constant shaking, and the left thinks they are supposed to ignore and not care about the shaking. Only the enlightened are awake, and only the awake are enlightened.

One day there will be none but Avatars. Every woman will be Laxmi and every man will be Laxmi

Narayan, Vishnu. One whole oneness will occur from all the ones, like an infinite rope that is made with infinite strings of ropes that are made with infinite strings of ropes and on. When each particle joins the whole creation and pronounces the sacred syllable AUM along with lord Brahma, the whole Maya will bow down to Laxmi Narayan and will find that it is Laxmi Narayan who bows unto them. Such is the unity of the two lovers.

23
It's All a Dream

This rope, the snake, is all a torus-like projection of Vishnu's dream. Like a part of the riverbank that is recessed in the land and becomes a little calm and swells around itself, this torus is where the flow of information forms a swell, which then swells back into its flow. It enters as Brahma and exits as Shiva. Just as a staircase has a turning point on each floor, so does the flow of information swell when it gets from zero to one.

This torus is Vishnu's dream pattern. It starts projecting when Vishnu moves his eyes in sleep and ends when he stops his eye movement.

The sages see this world as a dream that Vishnu projects. They do not interfere in his dream with their egoistic desires. They flow with the flow of the dream and know that, after all, it is just a dream. One who attains this level becomes free and gains inner peace. Such individuals worry about nothing, for they know Maya is nothing indeed.

They play, laugh, and cry but do not lose their identity in any of these forms. Just as butter never mixes with water, a sage never becomes entangled in the material and stays free and pure.

Vishnu dreams through our body, mind, and senses. What we see is what he dreams. So these eyes are made to dream. To become awake and see beyond this dreamworld, one needs to attain divine vision, the divine eyes that see through the reality of the dream, the truth that is running this whole show from behind the curtain.

Once you see the outer virtual world as absurd and in vain, you pursue the meaning and purpose of life from within. And you find a new world within yourself — you find the Self. For you come to the understanding that there is no meaning in mortality, and that the only immortal thing is consciousness. The consciousness that gives life to the lifeless.

To reach the source of consciousness, you must tear down the curtains in front of you. You must free yourself from your mind and senses, which are useful when dealing with stone and zeros. But when dealing with the formless, form is of no use. So you meditate and think and try to understand, feel, see, and hear, but beyond your mind and senses.

The seeker makes journeys beyond time and space, where there is pure information, consciousness, the seeker's own true Self, being, and source, which is Vishnu indeed. One who sees this truth loses interest in shadows and images. One who tastes spring water doesn't miss the taste of a pond of frogs and dragonflies. An eagle that knows how it feels to fly free does not prefer the comfort of being petted.

Seekers of the Self become the Self, for they are the ones who find. They asked for truth and found the Self, and indeed they found the truth. They now know the Kingdom of Heaven is nowhere but inside. They define themselves by themselves, not with anything outside of them. They find their center and balance in their eternal and immortal Self. They define themselves not with the mind or body. They know the body and mind are crystallized around the true Self. They know they are not anything perishable and mortal. That they are nothing that rots. There is nothing that can be contained in time and space. They contain time and space. They are the consciousness of information.

Be centered in your true Self. Dream your life on and manifest it, for you are the creator at work. You are the blessing and the giver of it to this world. You are the fountain of consciousness that nourishes and gives consciousness. Don't let your ego clog your flow.

To meditate is to journey in peace, data, and consciousness. But it is not easy. Many confuse it with relaxation of the mind and body. But it is a step toward the meditative state, where one is in trance. Once one relaxes the body and directs the intention from the outside to the inside world, one has levels to pass. It is a journey to Heaven through Hell. Hell is ego, fears, worries, attachments, false identity, darkness, lust, anger, and ignorance as a result of Earthly conditioning. Heaven is freedom, knowledge, peace, openness, consciousness, liveliness, light, and the Self.

Ego won't make it easy for beginners. Its fears and solidness and attachments turn their journeys into ordeals. One must push through this Hell. They will have to not give up and fail. It is not easy for the butterfly to tear up its cocoon and set itself free. But it will succeed, without a doubt. The Heaven of ignorance now becomes the Hell of demons. Now their eyes can see the walls of the cage of the ego made of attachments and desires. Demons will unsuccessfully try to keep them inside this cage.

Once they pass through this Hell, and the sound of *A* ends, they enter Purgatory. There, they hear the sound *U*. And they can go from one cell to another. They are wandering within the endless torus, the snake pattern, the labyrinth of creation. The snake of unlimited zeros, unlimited scales, unlimited eggs ready to be impregnated by the seed of Brahma, consciousness. But the seekers will find their way out when they finally become able to track the sound *M*. Thus, they level up.

When you vibe the same frequency as *M,* you can pass through the scales of the skin of the snake. You now see the snake from the outside, how endless it is, with unlimited scales, so colorful and constantly moving, like a spiral that has no end and no beginning. It ends where it begins and begins where it ends.

Now you have pronounced *AUM*, and have seen the creation from its lowest to its highest. *A* is the screaming sound of the wicked stone, the high frequency of the Self that won't pass through the shell of the ego of the stone; trapped in zero. *U* is the wondering sound of the amused, the medium frequency that shall pass from the cell of the ego and connect to the rest as one. And *M* is the sound of the whole, the base wave that can pass through all barriers of the labyrinth and at last through the outer skin of the snake to the higher dimension of information. The sound of the one snake of unlimited scales, scales in which form lives, the emptiness of matter waiting for the seeds of Brahma to bring them to life. *M* is the sound of wholeness, when these three stand together and become whole. Beyond whole is Vishnu. Their wholeness fades into the silence of consciousness, the pure consciousness of the meditative state of lord Vishnu.

In this dimension the whole torus of creation is so little, next to nothing.

24
Carnation
And
Reincarnation

The landing ones are the ones who incarnate.
They know why and from where they have come,
so they don't easily become entangled in the
Samsara Maya. They are always centered in the
Self and stay in consciousness. They are beyond
ego and their dharma is no dharma. They do
nothing personal, so they build no karma. And
when their body is of no more use and they have
done their divine tasks on Earth, they are ready to
go back and rejoice in pure consciousness.

It is the fallen ones who reincarnate, the ones who
have failed to keep oneness within and without,
those who have lost the Self and become all ego
and zeros.

When the body wears out, consciousness doesn't
know where to go; it leaves the current cell and
roams around within the snake until it germinates
within a cell of the torus. It is just a datum being
transferred from one unit to another, until it finds
the unit that can process it. It becomes processed
and finds a chance of being developed.

This process repeats itself until the data become
complete. And when complete data enter a unit,

the unit runs perfectly. That is when the zero is fully enlightened and the purpose of creation is accomplished. To make the zero full as one, like the creator. To become enlightened and conscious.

Now the seeker has experienced manifestation fully. There is nothing more to experience. But such individuals will be back on a mission, not out of confusion and immaturity, but with purpose. When their consciousness leaves their mortal body, they are ready to go back to their Heavenly abode.

One might ask, "Why so much headache for all this? Why all this drama and play?" That question is a game itself. Realize the game and you'll find the answer. Be neutral, stay centered and conscious; then you'll enjoy. Only the kids who take their game too seriously question why. Because when you take a game too seriously, you forget its truth, and you have to ask yourself why. Those who are illumined and know the reality of the game know the why of the game, and they enjoy it like a happy kid or wise adult.

25
Those Lost in Their Sleep
Dream Unconsciously

To be conscious when asleep and dreaming is very different from not being aware that you are asleep and in the dream state. That raises a similar question: Although we are alive, are we conscious that we are alive and living? How consciously are we living?

Imagine you are asleep and dreaming, and one of the characters in your dream asks if you are aware that you are really asleep and it is just a dream you're having. You might find that statement senseless if you are lost deep in your dreaming state. The enlightened one knows this is all Maya, knows it all just a dream. So think twice, and be not so sure this life is the whole truth; it might be just a dream, and truly it is.

Samsara Maya! The dream of the gods, which can be the nightmare of the ignorant ones. Be conscious that you are living in a dream. Be a dreamer. Be aware how free you are of all the attachments. All this Samsara is happening in Vishnu's mind.

The seeker who understands this feels reality at its deepest. The ignorant one, however, dwells on the surface only. The one who has come to this level of understanding feels wind as it is, hears sound as it is, and tastes food as it is, but the unconscious one, although doing the same things, never enjoys them as the enlightened one does.

Yes! The seeker sought the Self, found the Self, and became the Self. And it is by the Self and for the Self itself that this world has been created. And the Self is the only and ultimate enjoyer of this creation.

<u>26</u>
The Most Obvious Is
The Most Hidden
The Furthest From One Is
Nowhere Beyond the Self

We lose ourselves in the darkness of what we are ignorant of. And we seek on the outside of our ignorance. That is, we seek the lost Self in what we already know, for there is the light of knowledge. This is not wise seeking. We think to ourselves, it's too dark in the ignorance to find my mind. We would have to know we have to bring light to our darkness to be able to find the mind, to complete the whole Self. One can't run away from one's shadow toward light. The shadow will only enlarge as we run from it, in hope of approaching light. The only way to enlighten is to bring light into the darkness of the Self, and explore it. That is the way of the centered. One who does have the torch of consciousness in hand won't fear the darkest caves of the dragons of ignorance. Do not let the light be limited to the bright side, for the darkness will eat it. Do not let the darkness echo in itself and harden. Let the light in. Spread the light within. Light up.

The answer is within. Lighten the house and find your wealth within. You must first open a lock to access this treasure. It is a serpent made of a thousand heads that eat its thousand tails, a thousand mirrors and chambers, a moving infinite spiral that changes endlessly and rewrites its pattern like a fractal torus.

Vocalize *A* and recognize the darkness. Vocalize *U* and recognize the house. Say *M* and recognize the serpent. Say nothing and recognize the treasure.

Now you're about to see the truth. To see that it's always been, everywhere, just as silence is present everywhere and among all the sounds and voices, among all the rhythms and melodies and noises. Silence is the container of all waves. Wherever sound goes, silence was there first, and when sound is gone, silence will still be there. Time and place cannot be if there is not already information. From the information appears time and place.

Like an apple that everyone can see. Like the apple falling, which everyone can see. But also like the force that brings it down, which no one can see. Truth is so obvious and yet unseen to the eyes of those who do not seek, who are afraid of bringing the light of knowledge into their ignorance, so they can see what they have not yet seen.

Like the child of the seed-giving father and the birth-giving mother, like the consciousness that makes the child alive, truth is so obvious and yet is not seen by the eyes of the unconscious. The child and the mother and the father are seen, but the consciousness that makes them alive is unseen. The unconscious is no more than a stone, for both

the stone and the unconscious are unaware of
their own truth, lifeless and ignorant of the unseen
true meaning of life. Their awareness is limited to
the images and echoes.

27
To Be Is to Be the First
To Do Is to Do the Next
To Have Is the Last

One can neither do nor have without first being. Then one has existence and the capability of doing. Like a spiral that starts from the center of the tip of a needle, it is impossible to tell which comes right after the tip, to have or to do. But to be is the tip of the beginning, without a doubt. To be is the center, without a doubt. To be is Vishnu without a doubt.

The quiddity is the information, the life-giving pattern and paternal source that impregnates the maternal material. Then mother nature gives life to the new material being. And in this way, the creation begins and expands.

Brahma is a dot of Vishnu. A dot of consciousness echoes. From a dot came an echoed dot. They make a line. From the echo of the line appears another line and they make a surface. From the echo of the surface appears another surface, which makes a space. Space echoes itself and an echoed space appears. And the two of them make time. Space and time echo, and there appears an echo of space-time. And then information appears. This sacred fractal model is the shape of this world. The evolution of creation is to manifest the information, to become Self as whole. And that only happens through the creatures becoming whole from within. That way, Vishnu is reflected wholly and clearly in his own creation.

The demoniac have lost their centeredness and limp off their path. And eventually they become lost in the darkness. So ignorant do they become that they deny their own essence. They think of themselves as the doer and the haver, but not the be-er.

The quiddity is always true, but identity can be false. And one who identifies oneself without considering their quiddity is far from being alive and understanding life. For the quiddity is life itself. And dead are the ones who identify themselves with other than life. Zero is the one who doesn't count.

28
There Are Three Sciences
Two Are the Feet
One Is the Backbone

The knowledge of the Self is the backbone. One needs to be conscious and to know how to be conscious, to know who she is and what life and the purpose of life is.

The right foot is how to thrive as a whole, and the left foot is how to survive as an individual. The right foot is to actualize oneself, and the left is to indulge oneself. The former is how to serve others and the latter is how to make others serve us. One is how to be in harmony with nature and the other is how to manipulate it. One is how to give and the other is how to take. One is nursing and the other is exploiting.

Regardless of whether it is right or left, still it is paralyzed if doesn't have a healthy backbone. Love the love itself. Love your own Self. Love the Self of others. Be in love with love. Be the love. For with love comes openness to understanding. And with understanding comes openness to love.

Low is the knowledge of the dark. It is better than not having knowledge. It is not as good as having knowledge about what is immortal. It is instinct. It is not dark inside, but brings no light outside. It consumes and consumes and does nothing more than consume. That is the knowledge of the stone. It is a knowledge that guides a child's mouth to its mother's breast, or a sperm to an egg, but it cannot guide her to say a sentence by making sounds with her mouth. And it cannot guide one from her mortal life to immortality. The knowledge of the dark can't be taught or learned; it comes to you through nature. And finally, you leave it to nature.

The middle knowledge is also about mortality. It is better than instinct, but still dwells in the dark and will burn out. It brings light outside but cannot light a candle or a torch. It does not free a human being from mortal life. It tells someone how to be a better mortal. It tells a person how to make a phrase that makes sense. This knowledge doesn't come to you. You have to seek for it in nature. It won't make you immortal. But you can leave it to the other mortals when you leave.

The higher knowledge is the knowledge of the Self. It is the source of the knowledge that comes to you and that you also must come to. But this knowledge is the source of all other knowledge. It doesn't come to you, nor do you have to go to it. It is you. To learn that knowledge, you must know the Self. And to know the Self, you must become the Self. Each time you know the Self more, you become more the Self.

The domain of the Self is beyond instinct, intellect, and wisdom. They are merely the border between the dark and the light, like the shell of an egg. These are neither dividers nor connectors, and at the same time they are both.

To one on the right, the ego shell is left. That person sees it as a divider between herself and her source. To one who is on the left, the ego shell is right. It gives that individual the chance of material experience. And both of them are both right and wrong.

To one who is centered in the Self, who is beyond the duality defined by the ego, consciousness is all that matters. This individual doesn't have to try everything and see its failure. For now, he or she is situated beyond failure.

29
Fountain of Life

The living one seeks the truth, and the truth is oneness, oneness with the whole. But the door to infinity is nothingness. Just as your mother kicked you out of the heaven of her womb, your Self will kick you out of the Heaven of the ignorance of your ego. That is your spiritual birth. You are reborn into a new heaven.

The wholeness of the perfect circle of the whole creation was impregnated by consciousness, the source of love and life, Laxmi Narayan. Then it began to break up into pieces. Just as a tree has seeds, and each seed has trees within it, Brahma was given the seed and now gives the seed to the gods. Gods, having taken the seed, now pass it on to demigods, and so on, till a human being receives the seed of consciousness. And now it is the human being's duty to spread the seed of consciousness on Earth.

We must open the envelope and unfold the letter and reread what is written. Just as a magician throws an egg into the air and a pigeon appears on his hand, Vishnu threw a seed of life into the air, and a flower of life appears on his hand.

And it is the individual's job to turn this seed of consciousness into a flower. What has descended from the crown to the root now has to rise from the root to the crown. As the Self became ego, now that ego becomes the Self. The light hidden in the seed that was buried in the darkness under the ignorant ground now must rise, growing into the sky like a dawning sun. The tree of life raises its head.

For everything is from consciousness and everything goes back to consciousness, into the hat of the magician Vishnu.

30
Spiritual Orgy

Kali was asked, "Why so mad?"

"Because I am left alone," she replied. "All gods are in Heaven and all sages as well. The Earth is left full of the ignorant, who do no good. I am merely mirroring them back to themselves. I am the echo of their ego."

If none of the gods and demigods cares enough to take part in Vishnu's manifestation, then why should Kali care enough to be nice to it? Kali is to be praised, for at least she did not leave the Earth for Heavenly pleasures. If the gods and sages want Earth to be peaceful and happy, they need to land on Earth themselves and Selflessly stop enjoying the Heavenly joys. Then they will have to do good and help the Earth come into goodness. And Kali will reflect that accordingly.

Earth feels like Hell because all the good ones have gone to Heaven and are partying nonstop. And they have left the demons unwatched. Demoniacs are exchanging their consciousness for absurd mortal pleasures and falling into Hellish future reincarnations. They make Kali angry, and one who won't wake up with a nudge will be slapped, and one whom a slap won't awaken will receive even worse.

The Kalki Upanishad

The seed of consciousness in the world will flourish as the conscious individual. The one who is no more a slave of ego but its master glows with the light of knowledge of Self. That person becomes one. When all of humanity's egos become none and fill their nothingness with consciousness, they become as one. They become whole, like Brahma.

31
From the Exile of the Souls
To the Pilgrimage of the Souls

A king sent his ministers to find a land worthy of him, so that he could go and rule that city. They did so. Then he said, "Build there a city worthy to be my capital." They did so. Then he said, "Build a system of laws and rules worthy of a kingdom." And they did so. He said, "Select governors and staff worthy of serving my city." And they did. Then the king said, "I will rule only the worthy ones. So go and create citizens worthy of my kingdom."

But the ministers and princes went to the court of the king and said, "Oh lord, we tried and failed. For it is not possible to create a living being worthy of you, unless it's done by you."

The king said. "You can create a corpse, but you can't create consciousness. And yet, be not afraid, for now I put this mirror in their heart. They shall reflect me and be worthy of me. Hence, I may come down and rule them. The consciousness hidden in the seed that grows and turns a human being into a creature worthy of me is my very Self in them. Let this being be my image on Earth." And so he put mirrors in the streets and alleys and homes, which began to reflect him. And he said,

"All these images are me and I shall maintain their lives."

The era has just begun in which all beings become conscious of their selves. They connect to each other beyond their egos and become as one. They are Vishnu's incarnations. And they make this creation worthy of creation. They reflect Vishnu's pure consciousness and manifest Heaven on Earth, where the minus and the plus complete each other in harmony. Now they dance and do not fight. Now even the gods in Heaven envy the Earth, because the gods are limited to Heaven, but now humanity has both Heaven and Earth at the same time.

The enlightened ones have a mission now. They have done the first part, which is enlightenment and knowing the Self. Now they share this light and connect. Just as a butterfly's mission is to pollinate the blossoms once it's out of its cocoon, the enlightened ones must light the souls of others once they awaken as Vishnu.

It is a human being's job to gain Earthly pleasures and power but not be entangled with and attached to them. The ones on the right think that Earthly power and pleasures are to be denied. They are in the far darkness of the right side. That is an act of cowardliness, and now you will know why.

If one has no power to take revenge, there is not much value in that person's forgiving. But if one has the chance and the power to take revenge and doesn't, because she's free of ego's games and wants to forgive, then that is a godly act. Only the Self can do that, not an ego.

If you deny the Earthly sciences and businesses, you cause misery on Earth. And misery can never lead one to the Self, but only to darkness. It is far on the right in the darkness of the ego to deny one's Earthly duties even for Heavenly reasons.

Be centered in the center.

32
Enter the King

When we are done with the inner work and are fully conscious, we can start the outer work. One whose heart has not become fully aware of the Self may not lay even a brick to build the court of the lord on Earth. For such a person is not pure, and the court of the king can be built only by the hands of the pure.

All attempts to prepare for the king will become corrupt, if they are not already, because they were not made and maintained by the pure. How can we build the temple without first becoming pure inside? How can one with the darkness of ignorance within bring the light of consciousness to the outer world?

Those who have grown to adulthood but kept the inner child alive are worthy of raising children. Those who have grown out of the ego into the Self, and tamed the ego and brought it under their control, have attained enlightenment and are capable of spreading light in the outside world. Whether right or left, if they are not conscious and in the center, if they're not beyond their Earthly conditions, they may not spread light on Earth. For they are ignorant and in the darkness of their immature ego.

The conscious ones make this world divine. For they bring life and light with their presence. They make this Earth worthy of gods' landing. And once the enlightened ones populate, their king will land among them. They will become kings, shoulder to shoulder. Each desires to serve the other, and no one tries to rule the other. They dwell together in harmony. A true king is a server; a real king is a ruler. Two real kings are two egos — they may cease fire for a while, but they are never in peace. They can never be at the same time and place. Two true kings are two selves enlightened with consciousness. They will never fight but are always in harmony and peace. The whole creation and all its creatures will become the king as one, once they are illumined in knowledge.

Beware of the false and the lost.

33
God Demolishes the Devil as He Enters
God Enters as the Devil Is Demolished

If there is a false god, God won't enter that place. To do so, God must demolish the false ones, since the light is not in darkness unless the light demolishes it.

One must erase the falseness to empty the space for the truth. To become god, the enlightened one erased the false god, which is the ego. Thereupon that person's ego became the temple of the one consciousness. There is no more devil in the heart of such individuals. They are pure. They know they are gods, and gods are beyond ego. The ego is within the Self, the Self is not within the ego.

Demolish the gods of ignorance. Demolish the darkness. Be worthy of light, for he shows himself only to the pure ones. The god does not hang out with the lost and unconscious. Meditate and free your mind of all attachments, all boundaries, lust, and hunger and become rich in heart. Awaken your godself.

34
Who Ever Misses What
He Already Has?
Thus, the Devil Misses God

Once the enlightened one realizes her true Self, the Earthly manifestation no longer satisfies her. She sees the whole world as a small, suffocating cage. It might take her a while to realize that it's not separateness from the creator that is bothering her, for she is not separate. How can one be separate from the consciousness that exists everywhere and in everything? She will come to understand that it is the remains of her ego that make her feel like she's separated from the source. It is her own impurity that causes the darkness of ignorance and unconsciousness.

But the seeker will overcome this phase, too. For once a seeker, always a seeker. And a true seeker, a seeker of truth, won't give in to the illusion and darkness of the ego. Such persons seek until they find the truth and become the truth. For we cannot understand something fully until we possess that same quality. Until we realize that to understand the truth, we must become the truth. We have to find the true Self that makes us seek the truth. That is why we can't be satisfied with the mortal world, the world of shadows and images.

The Kalki Upanishad

The enlightened ones should not let their longing affect their material manifestation. For if they deny and reject their material existence, they commit an enormous sin. They cancel the whole progress they have made so far. The purpose of creation was for the individual to become the Maha Avatar. The holy actualization of the pure consciousness.

That is the center we have always been seeking. That is where everything finds balance, where left salutes right and right salutes left. One's mission on Earth is to become the Avatar, the embodiment of pure consciousness. The one who is the sweet fruit of the seed Vishnu handed to Brahma, which Brahma nurtured, and of which this world is the result.

The wise do not let the feeling of departedness from Heaven make them feel down. For how can one depart from what is everywhere and in everything? You are never truly departed from the divine Self. Instead, the wise become happy every time they feel departedness, for they know it is a sign of ego. Indeed, it is your ego that stands between you and your true Self.

Like a lover who sees the beloved and loses himself, the enlightened ones lose themselves in the moment of truth. The enlightened ones who dwell in nothing but truth have to maintain their alertness, or they will fail to function in the jungle of the ego. Even in a utopia, those intoxicated by the light of the Self must behave. For they must have reverence for the whole creation.

Walk on Earth with respect for her and all who are upon her. You are the Self. Act like it.

35
The Real Act of
The Doing One
And the True Intention
Of the Being One

One starts being a seeker of the truth because it feels strange to be anything or anyone other than one's true Self. At first, this feeling is unconscious. All one knows in the beginning is that something is wrong that makes everything feel not right.

One can be anything false in reality, but in truth one can't be anything other than one's true Self. It is that strange feeling of not being one's true Self, that awkward feeling of being lost, that makes one seek the Self and one's truth.

We all perform the act of becoming a being. We decide to be intentionally. We each pronounce I Am. And we are then reborn. One is, and then one knows that one is. You are completely aware of it. You don't live without being conscious that your heart is beating. You don't live like a corpse being driven around by your instincts. You see the corpse as dead. You see the Self as alive. You live because you know life now. You are a true living being who knows the Self, the true Self. You now know that life is nothing but consciousness. Now you are no longer a beast, but the god's very own Self.

Aum shanti shanti shanti.

Upcoming Works by Shahab Moradi

The Interpretation of the Yoga Sutras of Patanjali

The Interpretation of the Gospel of Thomas

The Interpretation of Tao Te Ching

The Interpretation of Bhagavad Gita